FAMILIES AROUND THE WORLD

A family from
GUATEMALA

Julia Waterlow

WAYLAND

FAMILIES AROUND THE WORLD

A family from **BOSNIA**

A family from **BRAZIL**

A family from **CHINA**

A family from **ETHIOPIA**

A family from **GERMANY**

A family from **GUATEMALA**

A family from **IRAQ**

A family from **JAPAN**

A family from **SOUTH AFRICA**

A family from **VIETNAM**

Cover: The Calabay family outside their home with all their possessions.
Title page: The Calabays stand in front of some of the bright cloth made and sold by the local people.
Contents page: Lucia washing the family's clothes at the side of Lake Atitlan.

Series editor: Katie Orchard
Designer: Tim Mayer
Production controller: Carol Titchener

Picture Acknowledgements: All the photographs in this book were taken by Miguel Luis Fairbanks. The photographs were supplied by Material World/Impact Photos and were first published by Sierra Club Books in 1994 © Copyright Miguel Luis Fairbanks/Material World. The map artwork on page 4 was produced by Peter Bull.

First published in 1997 by Wayland Publishers Limited
61 Western Road, Hove
East Sussex, BN3 1JD, England

© Copyright 1997 Wayland Publishers Limited

Find Wayland on the internet at http:///www.wayland.co.uk

Typeset by Mayer Media
Printed and bound by Canale & C. S.p.A., Turin, Italy.

British Library Cataloguing in Publication Data
Waterlow, Julia
  A family from Guatemala. – (Families around the world)
  1. Family – Guatemala – Juvenile literature
  2. Guatemala – Social life and customs – Juvenile literature
  I. Title
  306.8'5'097281

ISBN 0 7502 2026 0

Contents

Introduction

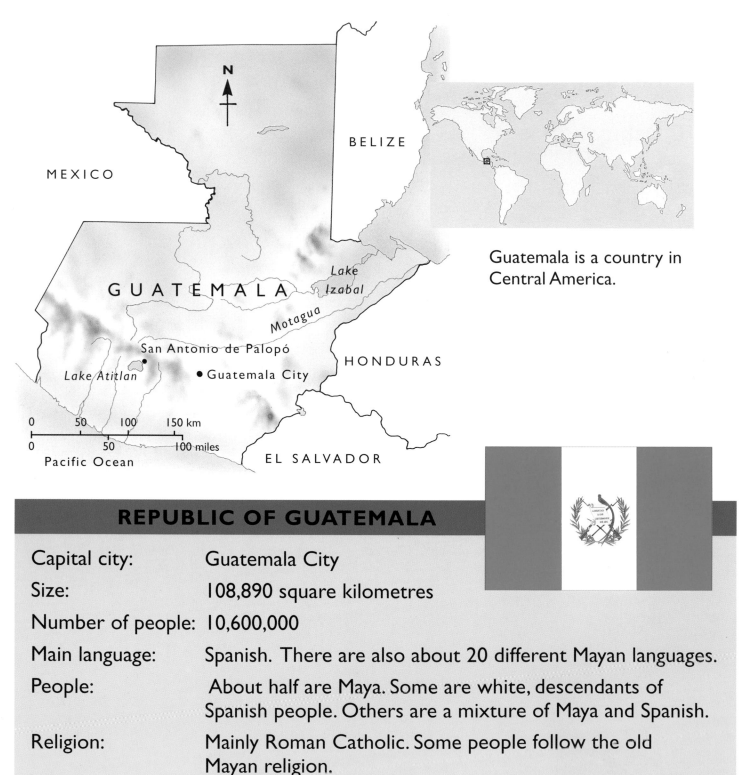

Guatemala is a country in Central America.

REPUBLIC OF GUATEMALA

Capital city:	Guatemala City
Size:	108,890 square kilometres
Number of people:	10,600,000
Main language:	Spanish. There are also about 20 different Mayan languages.
People:	About half are Maya. Some are white, descendants of Spanish people. Others are a mixture of Maya and Spanish.
Religion:	Mainly Roman Catholic. Some people follow the old Mayan religion.
Currency:	Quetzal

THE CALABAY FAMILY

Size of household:	5
Size of home:	20 square metres
Work week:	Vicente: 60 hours Lucia: 'constant!'
Most valued possessions:	Lucia: Religious painting Vicente: Cassette player Mario: Football
Family income:	US$994 each year

The Calabays are an ordinary Maya family who live in Guatemala. The Calabays have put everything that they own outside their home so that this photograph could be taken.

# Meet the family

1 Vicente, father, 29
2 Lucia, mother, 25
3 Mario, son, 8

4 Olivia, daughter, 6
5 Maria, daughter, 4

MAYAS

Maya people have lived in Guatemala for thousands of years. Some Guatemalans are a mixture of Spanish and Maya because the Spanish conquered Guatemala in 1523. Today, many people speak Spanish but the Maya have their own languages as well.

The Calabays live on the side of a hill, high up in the mountains of Guatemala. Below their house is their village, San Antonio de Palopó, and a lake, Lake Atitlan. The Calabay family has always lived here, farming small plots of land to grow their food.

'It doesn't take us long to walk down to the village, but coming up the hill again is hard work when we're carrying things.' *Vicente.*

The Calabay house

On the side of the house is a little shed. Inside is the newest thing the Calabays own – a smart white toilet.

A Home of Their Own

The Calabays saved up to buy their own house. It is made of mud bricks and has a tin roof. They have one room inside which Vicente has painted white to make it bright and cheerful. The family also has a small building beside the house, where they cook and store their food. They don't have a tap, so Lucia collects water in big plastic containers. The family usually goes down to the lake to wash.

'We have one room which we use for weaving, eating and sleeping in.' *Lucia.*

The Calabays don't have a lot of things in the house. There are a few bits of furniture, their clothes, the looms they use for weaving and tools for farming – all things that they can't do without. But they do have a radio cassette player and a few toys for the children to play with.

The Calabays have a bed, a table and a mat on the floor. Lucia has decorated the walls with some pictures.

▲ At night, the children curl up together with their toys.

Tucked up Safe at Night

The Calabays all sleep together in their one room. The children sleep on a mat on the floor, and Vicente and Lucia have a bed. To be on the safe side, they lock the door at night to keep out bandits or thieves. But no one has ever tried to break in.

Cooking and eating

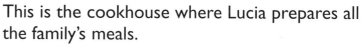

TASTY *TORTILLAS*

In Guatemala, people eat *tortillas* rather than bread. *Tortillas* (you say tor-tee-yas) are made of flour and water mixed together. The mixture is rolled out into thin, round pancakes and cooked in a big, flat pan over the fire.

This is the cookhouse where Lucia prepares all the family's meals.

Tortillas

Lucia puts a big pan on the fire, puts in a little oil and fries the *tortillas*. The Calabays have *tortillas* with all their meals.

'I eat *tortillas* for breakfast, lunch and dinner.' *Maria*.

Maria and Lucia are in the cookhouse making lunch.

Lucia cooks the family's meals on a fire in the corner of their cookhouse. She has made the fireplace out of stones and puts her cooking pots on top. Lucia hangs her pans and baskets on the walls when she's not using them.

The cookhouse doesn't have a chimney, so the smoke from the fire makes the walls of the cookhouse rather black. Lucia kneels on a mat to keep her clothes clean.

Hot and Spicy

The Calabays grow most of the food they eat. They go to the market in the nearby town of Solola to buy food they can't grow themselves. Lucia uses flour made out of maize to make *tortillas* and *tamales*. Often Lucia adds chillies to the food, which makes it hot, but tasty.

At breakfast, the family sometimes has scrambled eggs. At midday, they often eat beans and rice. In the evening, one of their favourite meals is beans and *tamales*. And, of course, with every meal they have *tortillas*!

The local market sells all kinds of fruit and vegetables.

Lucia is making *tamales*, which are like cakes made of flour with a spicy filling. She wraps them up in leaves and steams them.

Working hard

FARMING THE LAND

Most people in Guatemala are farmers. They grow enough food to feed their families, and sometimes a little extra to sell at the market. A few Guatemalans work for big landowners, who grow crops such as coffee and bananas.

The Calabay family has two looms and a spinning wheel. Vicente uses the largest loom to weave blankets.

Weaving

Vicente weaves blankets for the village shop. The shelves of brightly coloured blankets reach right up to the ceiling. Many tourists visit Lake Atitlan and they buy blankets to take home as souvenirs.

'It takes me several days to weave one blanket.' *Vicente.*

Vicente hoes the ground, ready for planting more vegetables.

Farming

Vicente is also a farmer. He works with a few simple tools, such as the hoe he uses to clear his fields of weeds. He also has three very sharp machetes for cutting down tough plants. Vicente walks every day to work on fields on the slopes rising up from the lake. Mario sometimes goes with his father to watch and learn.

Housework

After each meal, Lucia washes up the pots and pans with water she has fetched from the lake. If the weather is fine, she likes to do this outside.

'Jon Pipin', the family pet turkey, watches Lucia wash up to see if there are any scraps of food.

Lucia keeps very busy looking after the family. Apart from washing the dishes, she chops up wood for the fire every day. Lucia also goes down to the lake to collect water or wash the clothes.

Lucia washes the family's clothes in the lake. It's hard work, but there is a beautiful view of the mountains.

Things to Sell

There is always plenty for Lucia to do. Lucia and her friends sometimes sort the onions they have grown. They tie them into neat bundles, ready for sale at the market in Solola. When Lucia has some spare time, she uses the spinning wheel or the smaller of the two looms. She makes wristbands and bags to sell to tourists.

Lucia plaits onions into bundles to take to market and catches up on the local gossip.

School and play

These are the children's favourite toys.

Most children in Guatemala go to primary school, but not many go on to secondary school. A lot of families don't have enough money. They need their children to help work on the land when they get older.

Learning to Read

Mario and Olivia go to the local school in San Antonio. They walk together down the hill to school early in the morning. Lucia is glad that her children are learning to read and write. Vicente can read and write, but Lucia never went to school.

'Mum says I shouldn't play football inside, but I do anyway.' *Mario*.

Football Crazy

If it's wet outside after school, the children play inside the house. They don't have a television but they find other things to do, such as drawing. The girls have fun playing with their dolls. Mario is mad about football. He spends nearly all his spare time kicking or heading his ball around.

▼ Mario and his classmates at school.

Spare time

▶ The radio cassette player is very important to Vicente.

▼ Vicente catches up on the local news.

SPORT

Football is the main sport played in Guatemala. Many children also learn to play basketball at school.

Time to Relax

Vicente and Lucia don't have much time to sit down and relax. But if Lucia's friends drop in while she's doing something, she always stops for a chat. Vicente loves listening to the radio when he's not working. Sometimes he sits down and reads the local newspaper.

'I often fall asleep on the bus on the way to market.' *Olivia.*

Off to Market

The Calabays travel on a bus to the market.

The Calabays go to market once a week. They go to Solola, which isn't far away. The road is a bit bumpy so it can take the bus an hour to get there. Lucia does her weekly food shopping there.

A Religious Family

Lucia is very religious. She often goes to pray at an altar to the village saint, San Antonio del Monte. On the altar there are candles, religious pictures and flowers. Each year a different family in the village is allowed to have the altar in their house. Lucia believes that the saint looks after their village.

RELIGION

Guatemalan people are Christian. There are churches in nearly all towns and villages. Some Maya also pray to their own gods of rivers, mountains, rain and corn.

Lucia and other villagers pray at this altar. It is kept at a neighbour's house.

'Our biggest festival is our saint's day in June. Everyone comes out on the streets to watch the colourful parades.' *Lucia.*

The future

Vicente and Lucia would like the children to stay at school for many more years. But as soon as Mario, Olivia and Maria are old enough, their parents will need them to help with all the work. Mario wants to be a farmer and weaver like his father.

The Calabays are happy with their work and way of life. Of course, it would be nice to have more money. Most of all, they would like a television.

Mario likes reading. But he will soon have to leave school to help his father.

'It would be nice to have some new things for the house.' *Lucia.*

Timeline

2000 BC	Maya people fish and farm the land.
400–900 AD	The Mayan civilization is at its greatest. The Maya build cities and temples.
1523	Spanish soldiers sail across the Atlantic and conquer Guatemala. Many Maya are killed.
1821	Guatemala becomes an independent country. Rich landowners control the country. The Maya remain poor.
1951–1984	Strong and cruel leaders rule Guatemala, killing those who don't agree with them. Poor Guatemalans try to fight the government. Many die during the troubles.
1986 and 1991	There are elections. New leaders promise to try and bring peace. But there is still some fighting, and the government finds it difficult to keep law and order.

Glossary

Altar A table with religious things on it where people come to pray.

Chillies Small vegetables with a very hot taste.

Christian Someone who follows the religious teachings of Jesus Christ.

Elections These are when people vote to choose their new leaders.

Independent country A country that rules itself and is not controlled by another country.

Looms Wooden frames that are used for weaving.

Machetes Sharp, heavy knives used for cutting down plants.

Maize A cereal crop. Some types of maize can be dried and ground up to make flour.

Spinning wheel A special wheel used to make long threads out of wool.

Volcanoes Cone-shaped hills or mountains where hot rocks from deep under the earth have pushed up violently to the surface.

Weaving Making cloth by threading strands of cotton in and out of each other.

Further information

Books to read:

Books for younger readers about Guatemala are difficult to find. You might like to read *Look into the Past – the Maya* by Peter Chrisp (Wayland, 1994) which tells you about the Maya people in the past.

Organizations:

The following organizations have a selection of education packs, some of which include case studies of children around the world:

Action Aid, Chataway House, Chard, Somerset TA20 1FA Tel: 01460 62972

Oxfam, 274 Banbury Road, Oxford OX2 7DZ Tel: 01865 311311

Save the Children, 17 Grove Lane, London SE5 8RD Tel: 0171 703 5400

Index